Simone K. Busch

von Schatten trinken
sipping from shadows

Haiku

Bibliographische Information der Deutschen Nationalbibliothek: Die Deutsche Nationalbibliothek verzeichnet diese Publikation in der Deutschen Nationalbibliografie; detaillierte bibliografische Daten sind im Internet über http//dnb.dnb.de abrufbar.

*©2017 Simone K. Busch
Konzept, Layout & Fotos: Simone K. Busch, Rheinbach
Herstellung und Verlag: Books on Demand, Norderstedt*

ISBN 9783743143401

Für C., M. und A.

„Man muss weggehen können
und doch sein wie ein Baum:
als bliebe die Wurzel im Boden,
als zöge die Landschaft und wir ständen fest. ..."

"We must be able to go away
and yet be like a tree:
rooted in the earth
standing fast while the landscape passes. ..."

Ziehende Landschaft*/Passing Landscapes, Hilde Domin

*aus: Hilde Domin, Sämtliche Gedichte, 3. Aufl. 9, 2019, S. Fischer Verlag GmbH, S. 10

Einführung

Nach der Lektüre dieses Buches (Haiku-Bandes) fragen sich die Leser, ob die vier Jahre Aufenthalt in Japan Simone K. Busch nicht ebenso stark geprägt haben, wie die Zeit in Deutschland. In Ihren Texten erzählt sie von ihren Erfahrungen, ihren Begegnungen mit den stillen und lauten Momenten einer Millionenmetropole, vom Aufeinandertreffen von Tradition und Moderne und vom Zauber einer Kultur, die ihr in den Jahren ihres Japanaufenthaltes nicht mehr fremd ist und in die sie uns mit offenen Armen (im Kimono) willkommen heißt.

Aber Simone K. Busch verschweigt eben auch nicht ihre tiefe Sehnsucht nach der Heimat. Und so ist in ihren Haiku oft von Heimat, heimgekehrt und Heimweh die Rede.
In einer poetischen Aufarbeitung und Rückbesinnung stellt sich auf jeder Seite ihres Haiku-Bandes die Frage: Wo ist ihre Heimat?

> ein Ginkgo Blatt-
> zerrissen zwischen Heimat
> und Zuhause

Wie selbstverständlich ist für die Haiku-Dichterin die Einbindung der sogenannten Gendai-Haiku. Ihre Texte sind nicht mehr nur in der sogenannten traditionellen Struktur (*dentô*) geschrieben, sondern frei komponiert.

In ihren zeitgenössischen Haiku geht es darum, einen Augenblick in der Natur und in ihrem gesellschaftlichen bzw. geschichtlichen Umfeld zu beschreiben. Bei einem Besuch des Friedensdenkmals in Hiroshima entstand dieses Haiku

> Atom-Dom
> die Trauer schlucken
> rote Azaleen

Da alle Texte für eine breitere Leserschaft in deutscher und englischer Sprache vorliegen, hier zwei Beispiele, in denen die Haiku Poetin das Ungesagte gekonnt auch in der englischsprachigen Version auf uns wirken lässt.

> sudden gust
> a child carries blossoms
> into the future

In dem Haiku

> Metro station
> a butterfly opens
> a girl's mouth

beschreibt Simone K. Busch den Augenblick des Staunens eines Mädchens über die Schönheit der Natur in einer eher technischen Umgebung.

Das Haiku erschließt sich nicht immer auf den ersten Blick, sondern im Erleben des wohl komponierten Nachhalls (*yoin*), der den Text beim Betreten der neuen Ebene erst zum Haiku macht. Wie diese Beispiele zeigen, muss der Gebrauch eines *kigo* nicht grundsätzlich ausgeklammert werden, sondern kann einen deutlichen Bezug auf eine Jahreszeit nehmen.

Auf ihren Reisen durch Japan hatte Simone K. Busch einen intensiven Kontakt mit den religiösen Konzepten des Buddhismus

und Shintoismus. In ihren Haiku bilden daher die Natur, das gesellschaftliche Sein auf der einen Seite und die Dichterin im beobachteten Augenblick ein dynamisches Ganzes. Diese Dynamik steht für das nichtsagbare *Mu*.
Diese Leere und das Nicht-offen-Zutagetreten des Schönen ist ein wichtiger Teil der japanischen Ästhetik. Simone K. Busch geht es in ihren Texten also auch darum stets einen Rest ungesagt zu lassen und nicht alles offen auszusprechen.

    alles ist möglich
in diesem leeren Raum
    Grillenorchester

    voller Mond
hineingezogen ins Nichts
   des Japanpapiers

Morgenhaut
das Wasser des Sees
ohne Alter

so auch im folgenden Haiku

tausche ein Lächeln
mit dem Mönch vom Berg
Pfirsichbaum in Blüte

Dieses Haiku lebt von der Flüchtigkeit und dem Besonderen des Augenblicks (*yûgen*). Wären Beide stehen geblieben und hätten ein paar Worte gewechselt, wäre der leere Raum (*yohaku*) besetzt worden und die Offenheit des Textes wäre verloren gegangen. Die zeitlose Stille wird in diesem Haiku festgehalten.

Eine wichtige Erfahrung aus der Zeit in Japan ist die Kenntnis der japanischen Sprache, die in einige ihrer Texte wie unabsichtlich einfließt. Die Liebe der Autorin zu Gestaltung von Haiga (Bild- und Textkompositionen) finden wir in den grandiosen schwarz-weiß Grafiken wieder, die – wie das Haiku – den Lesern den Freiraum bieten, in die Assoziationswelt der Autorin zu treten, um das zu entdecken, was im Text und im Bild eben nicht ausgesprochen wurde.

Am Ende schließt sich der Kreis über das Jagen roter Blätter zum roten Ahorn, der unser Leben beleuchtet. Die Lektüre dieses Buches ist ein großes Vergnügen, nicht nur für Haiku-Poeten.

Gerd Börner
Berlin im Dezember 2016

Foreword

Several years ago, a lady called Simone started attending the Meguro International Haiku Circle in Tokyo, of which I was moderator. Several years later, she has created this intriguing book of haiku and honored me with an invitation to write a foreword.

I would like to take advantage of this opportunity to explore a question, which has occupied my mind for a number of years, namely, what distinguishes an excellent haiku from a mediocre one? The plethora of excellent haiku in this collection affords ample chance to begin answering this question. Needless to say, it is a question with more than one answer.

The first haiku that I would like to draw the reader's attention to is:

> foggy mountain road
> a monkey on the guardrail
> foggy mountain road

In my opinion, this is an excellent haiku, not because it has a 5-7-5 syllabic structure, but because of the effective use of repetition in the first and third lines, which conveys the monotony of driving on a foggy mountain road, monotony broken by the monkey in the second line, only to be quickly resumed in the third line. The haiku continues beyond itself in that the reader is led to believe that the foggy mountain road will continue until another monkey appears, to again punctuate the monotony. The fact that the monkey is stationary and being quickly left behind creates the sensation of speed so that the reader experiences the haiku as a passenger in the vehicle. In brief, this haiku is a glorious example of how the technique of repetition can be utilized, even in a genre as short as haiku, to very great effect.

The next haiku, which I would like to throw the spotlight on is:

> the way
> he's asking my name
> warm sake

This haiku's excellence might be attributed to two factors. The first is the "space between the lines" or 行間 (gyoukan) in Japanese; and the second is the effective employment of a season word. The 行間 is what we do not say in words but as a nuance it is nonetheless there, enticing the reader to interpret it. The first and second lines have a 行間 in that "the way he's asking my name" is not described. However, what really brings this 行間 to life is the season word "warm saké" in the third line. The third line ignites the 行間 of the first two lines, unlocking possible interpretations, such as warm saké might be having a romantic effect on both characters featured in the haiku, or warm saké might be causing one of the characters to misconstrue the intentions of the other. By setting up this kind of interaction between 行間 and season word, Simone has created a haiku which really has the power to enthrall the reader.

While technique is important in creating an excellent haiku, so also is the theme itself. One theme that I have observed in this collection is discrepancy, for instance, between the physical and the emotional, or between the superficial and the underlying. Discrepancy is a theme that lends itself well to haiku, having the potential to instantly arrest or even shock the reader. Two examples from this collection are:

> rush hour
> by 1000 touches
> untouched

> deep red sun
> a bell boy bows
> at the shuttle bus

The discrepancy in the first haiku is clear, stark even. This haiku arrests by showing us the extent to which modern life has contributed to the discrepancy between our physical and emotional worlds. The theme of people touching without feeling is surely one that is reminiscent of Paul Simon's classic "The Sound of Silence".

The second haiku is very much a "photographic haiku". Taken at face value, this is an everyday scene at hotels throughout Japan. What is striking is the absurdity of bowing at a shuttle bus, which leads us to consider what the bell boy is really doing, and what we are really witnessing here. The bell boy's bow is of course an expression of respect and gratitude to the travelers who have been guests at his hotel and who are now departing; but more than that, the bow is a manifestation of the discrepancy or mismatch between the traditional and the modern, which in effect testifies to the resilience of Japanese traditional customs in the midst of a modern world that is littered with obstructions to tradition, such as shuttle buses. The discrepancy here is between the superficial absurdity and the underlying respectability of this scene.

Whether you are about to read this book of haiku for sheer enjoyment or have a mind to pick up some tips about writing haiku yourself, or indeed, if you are keen to glean some insight into life in Japan, read on! You will not be disappointed.

Catherine Urquhart
Founder, Edinburgh Haiku Circle, December 2016

die Schichten des Seins

the layers of being

eine Rakete
entflammt im Nebel
Kamelienblüten

a rocket
inflaming in the mist
camellia flowers

Kondensstreifen
die Spanne zwischen Heimat
und Zuhause

vapour trails
the span between homeland
and home

drifting alone
through the unknown town –
my forgotten smile

allein
durch die unbekannte Stadt –
mein vergessenes Lächeln

most silent hour
at night near the graveyard
plum blossom scent

zur stillsten Stunde
nachts nahe beim Friedhof
Pflaumenblütenduft

Nebelberge
erwache in einem Bild
von Yosa Buson

misty mountains
waking up in a picture
of Yosa Buson

googleblau
der Punkt dem ich folge
bin ich

googleblue
the dot i am following
is me

metro station
a butterfly opens
a girl's mouth

U-Bahnstation
ein Schmetterling öffnet
einen Mädchenmund

gegenüber
der Fremde spricht
Heimat

opposite
the stranger speaks
homeland

Langstreckenflug
in der Fremde warte ich
auf mich

long distance flight
i wait in the foreign land
for me

Yamanote Line
meine Angst
Millionen Jahre alt

Yamanote Line
my fear
millions of years old

Rushhour
von 1000 Berührungen
unberührt

rush hour
by 1000 touches
untouched

voll von Worten
vergangener Nächte
Sakura Mond

filled with words
of bygone nights
sakura moon

heiliger Berg
im Dämmer der Reispapierwand
Nachbars Furz

sacred mountain sleeps
behind the rice paper wall
neighbour's fart

eBook
ein Hauch von Pflaumenblüten
Jahrhunderte alt

ebook
a whiff of plum blossoms
centuries old

Stromtrasse
Fischadler nisten
im Wind

electric line
ospreys nesting
in the wind

kimono fitting
the layers of being
easily shed

Kimono Anprobe
die Schichten des Seins
einfach ablegen

Maulbeerseide
die Zungenspitze
des Malers tanzt

mulberry silk
the tip of the artist's tongue
dances

blossoms at their peak
booking a one-way flight
to my homeland

Kirschbaumblüten
buchen ein One-Way Ticket
in die Heimat

Frühlingsgras
die Träume der Krieger
in den Kindern

spring grasses
the dreams of warriors
within children

beschwingt
vor dem Premium Outlet—
Bettelglöckchenklang

elated
in front of the premium outlet—
a beggar monk rings his bell

sudden gust
a child carries blossoms
into the future

plötzlicher Wind
ein Kind trägt Kirschblüten
in die Zukunft

Kamikaze Museum
eine Kamelienknospe entfaltet
ihre Wahrheit

kamikaze museum
a camellia bud unfolding
its truth

swapping smiles
with a mountain monk
peach tree in bloom

tausche ein Lächeln
mit dem Mönch vom Berg
Pfirsichbaum in Blüte

Meerenge

strait

Sonnenaufgang
ein paar Kiesel am Strand
krabbeln fort

sunrise
pebbles on the beach
scuttle away

Meerenge
die Uberflugrechte
der Möwen

strait
the flyover rights
of gulls

Atom-Dom
die Trauer schlucken
rote Azaleen

atomic dome
absorbing the sorrow
red azaleas

Schattenblätter
auf der hölzernen Wand
Nagasaki Tag

shadows of leaves
on the wooden wall
Nagasaki Day

Friedensstatue
eine Taube trinkt
vom Schatten

peace statue
a dove sipping
from the shadow

the child
behind the warrior
fireflies

das Kind
hinter dem Krieger
Leuchtkäfer

Familientreffen
die dunklen Fäden
im All

family reunion
the dark filaments
in space

die Kinder sind fort
in den Händen der Saft
von weißem Pfirsich

children left
in my hands the juice
of white peaches

Kriebelmücken
in der Nacht die Bisse
eines alten Traums

black flies
at night the bites
of an old dream

Sutren kopieren
von links nach rechts
das Morgenlicht

copying sutra
from left to right
the morning light

alles ist möglich
in diesem leeren Raum
Grillenorchester

the sky is the limit
in this empty room
orchestra of crickets

Shinkansen
ziehe den Rotz hoch
wie mein Nachbar

Shinkansen
i sniff back the snot
like my neighbour

Bonsai-Show
mein Kind lassen
wie es ist

bonsai show
leaving my child
as she is

im kleinen Garten
noch kleiner ich
geborgte Landschaft

in the small garden
the smaller me
borrowed landscape

sleepy pond
touched by the sound
of an old frog

schläfriger Teich
berührt vom Geräusch
eines alten Froschs

Morgenhaut
das Wasser des Sees
ohne Alter

morning skin
the water of the lake
without age

zurück zum Yoga
mein Körper löst sich
von der Zeit

back to yoga
my body frees itself
from time

der Fluss
treibt weiter im trockenen Bett
Ainu Musik

the river
drifting onwards in its dried-out bed
Ainu music

Heimaturlaub
abseits im Gespräch
mit den Schwalben

home leave
chatting aside
with swallows

Regentag
ich weiß vom Amselgesang
im geheimen Garten

all day rain
i know of blackbirds singing
in the secret garden

alter Tempel
eine Regenkette spielt
Schönberg

ancient temple
a rain chain playing
Schönberg

Lavendelduft
ihre Augen auf dem Selfie
geschlossen

scent of lavender
her eyes in the selfie
closed

einen Spritzer Yuzu

a dash of yuzu

Was ist Heimat?
in mein deutsches Gericht
einen Spritzer Yuzu

what is homeland?
into my German dish
a dash of yuzu

allein unterwegs
eine Handvoll Wärme
vom Maronenmann

travelling alone
a handful of warmth
from the chestnut vendor

a white heron
reflected in the cold river
homeless blue

ein weißer Reiher
spiegelt sich im kalten Fluss
heimatloses Blau

rain on rain
sun yellow the cape
of a dachshund

Regen auf Regen
das Cape eines Dackels
sonnengelb

Taifun ...
über den Trümmern der Duft
grüner Orangen

typhoon ...
a scent of green oranges
above the debris

rote Blätter jagen
die Stille des Fuji

red leaves chasing
the silence of Mount Fuji

taking a rest
at the desk of Shiki
autumn butterfly

innehalten
am Schreibtisch von Shiki
ein Herbstschmetterling

Erntezeit
ein Kind im Rollstuhl
sammelt Licht

harvest time
a child in a wheelchair
gathering light

Gänse ziehen
wir teilen unsere Träume
mit dem Wind

geese depart
we share our dreams
with the wind

unterm blauen Himmel
der blaue Himmel
des Obdachlosen

under the blue sky
the blue sky
of the rough sleeper

Marktfeilscherei
in den Augen des Thunfischs
noch Meer

bargaining
in the eyes of the tuna
still some sea

autumn breeze
our words at the pond
meet and part

Herbstbrise
unsere Worte am Teich
treffen und trennen sich

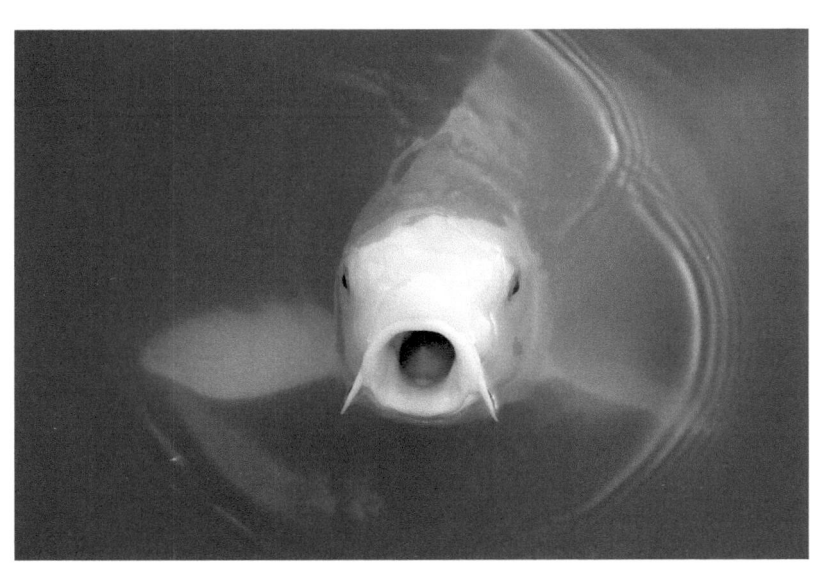

Herbstwellen
die Leere
in meinem Schoß

autumn waves
the vacancy
inside my womb

Nirwana Blume
darauf ein Schmetterling
den ich niemals sah

nirvana flower
thereupon sits a butterfly
i have never seen

kalter Niesel
füllt den Trockengarten
mit Leere

cold drizzle
filling the rock garden
with emptiness

a ginkgo leaf –
torn between homeland
and home

ein Ginkgo Blatt –
zerrissen zwischen Heimat
und Zuhause

roter Ahorn
am Abend beleuchtet
dieses kurze Leben

red maple
lit-up at night
this short life

kalte Sternennacht
ein Zikadenlied
wird Traum

cold starry night
a cicada's song
turns into a dream

foggy mountain road
a monkey on the guardrail
foggy mountain road

Nebelbergstraße
ein Affe auf der Leitplanke
Nebelbergstraße

voller Mond
hineingezogen ins Nichts
des Washi Papiers

full moon
drawn into the vastness
of washi paper

balancing
between effort and ease
autumn reflections

balancierend
zwischen Mühe und Erleichterung
Herbstgedanken

wir teilen die Dunkelheit

we share the darkness

grinding my thoughts
the fragrance
of roasted sesame

meine Gedanken mahlen
der Duft
von geröstetem Sesam

Hunger
im Bauch von Buddha
knurrt ein Handy

hunger
in the belly of Buddha
a mobile rumbles

snow moon
we share the darkness
of pumpernickel

Schneemond
wir teilen die Dunkelheit
von Pumpernickel

1000 Stufen ...
für einen Atemzug erleuchtet
der Bergtempel

1000 steps ...
for one enlightened breath
the mountain temple

little snail
in my hand – too late to climb
Mount Fuji

kleine Schnecke
in meiner Hand – zu spät
für die Fuji-Besteigung

hot spring
snow monkeys at play
with my inner child

heiße Quelle
Schneeaffen spielen
mit meinem inneren Kind

longest night
balancing his words
in a brushstroke

längste Nacht
seine Worte balancieren
im Pinselstrich

Schneesturm
im Zentrum der Stadt
der leere Raum

snow storm
in the city centre
empty space

wie er fragend
meinen Namen sagt
warmer Sake

the way
he's asking my name
warm sake

frostiger Wind
eine Handvoll Briefe
hinaus in die Welt

bleak wind
a handful of letters
out into the world

Morgenschnee
die alte Pinie
erfindet sich neu

morning snow
the old pine tree
reinvents itself

icy moon
i start talking
to a calla lily

eisiger Mond
ich beginne das Gespräch
mit einer Calla

Partitur von 4'33''-
vor dem Museum
fällt Schnee

score of 4'33''-
outside the museum
falling snow

Wintersonnenwende
ich trinke das Licht
einer Orange

midwinter
sipping the light
from an orange

Christmas Day
bathing in the hot spring
my homesickness

Weihnachtstag
tauche in die heiße Quelle
mein Heimweh

rote Sonne
ein Page verneigt sich
am Shuttle Bus

deep red sun
a bell boy bows
at the shuttle bus

Winternacht
3 Wünsche in die Schale
des Mondes

winter's night
3 wishes into the bowl
of the moon

heimgekehrt
aus der Erde ragen
rote Wurzeln

returned home
red roots sticking out
of the soil

leere Zikade
im nächsten Leben
bin ich frei

empty cicada
next life
i will be free

Für die, die fragen

Ainu, Ureinwohner Nordjapans. *Ainu* bedeutet „Mensch" in *Ainu*-Sprache
Geborgte Landschaft, *‚shakkei'*, beschreibt, wie die Aussicht zum Bestandteil einer Gartenkomposition wird
Heiße Quelle, *‚onsen'*, Ort mit Hotels, die über ein von natürlichen heißen Quellen gespeistes Bad verfügen
Kamikaze, oder **Shimpū Tokkōtai** waren Selbstmordangriffe der japanischen Kaiserlichen Marineluftwaffe gegen die Kriegsschiffe der Alliierten im Endstadium des Pazifikkrieges im 2. Weltkrieg
Kimono, wortwörtlich „Anziehsache", ein traditionelles, kaftanartiges Kleidungsstück, das durch einen breiten Gürtel (*‚obi'*) zusammengehalten wird. Unter dem sichtbaren Kimono werden verschiedene Unterkleider getragen.
Nirvana Blume, eine Liliensorte, die im September in Japan blüht, jap. *‚higanbana'*, auf Deutsch ‚Blume vom anderen Ufer'. ‚Das andere Ufer' ist Nirvana, wo weltliche Dinge verlöschen und ersetzt werden durch Erleuchtung und nichtmaterieller Existenz
4'33" (*Four minutes, thirty-three seconds*), ein Musikstück des Avantgarde-Komponisten John Cage, bei dem kein einziger Ton gespielt wird
Reispapierwand, verschiebbare Raumteiler, die in der traditionellen Architektur Japans Verwendung finden. Sie können die Funktion von Außenwänden, Türen oder Raumteilern übernehmen.
Pflaumenblüten, gemeint ist die stark duftende *‚ume'*, die japanische Aprikose oder Pflaume.
Sake, bezeichnet im allgemeinen jede Form von Alkohol in Japan. Nicht-Japaner verstehen darunter meist den japanischen Reiswein.
Schönberg, Arnold (1874 – 1951) österreichisch-amerikanischer Komponist und zentrale Figur der „Wiener atonalen Schule" in die Zwölftontechnik mündete.
Masaoka Shiki, (1867-1902) japanischer Dichter, Schriftsteller, Literaturkritiker und Essayist der Meiji-Zeit, Begründer der modernen Haiku-Dichtung und neben Buson, Issa und Bashô einer der vier großen Haiku-Meister
Shinkansen, sowohl Name des Streckennetzes japanischer Hochgeschwindigkeitszüge als auch Bezeichnung für die Züge selbst
Sutra, wörtlich ‚Faden' oder ‚Kette', sind elementarste Texte des Buddhismus mit Merksatz-Charakter.
Trockengarten, *‚karesansui'*, eine Sonderform des japanischen Gartens, der nur aus Kies, Steinen und Felsbrocken besteht. Mit Ausnahme von Moos werden keine Pflanzen verwendet. Wasser ist durch wellenförmige Strukturen in Kies- oder Sandflächen angedeutet.
Washi, handgeschöpftes, durchscheinendes Papier aus Japan. Es wird aus Bastfasern von Gehölzen niedriger Wuchshöhe (z.B. Gampi und Kozo) gewonnen.
Yamanote Line, Ringbahnlinie in Tôkyô und eine der wichtigsten und am meisten frequentierten Bahnstrecken in der Stadt.
Yosa Buson, (1716-1784) der Dichter-Maler unter den großen Haiku-Meistern
Yuzu, hellgelbe bis orangefarbene, in Japan gebräuchliche Zitrusfrucht. Sie ähnelt der Zitrone, hat aber ein wesentlich komplexeres Aroma.

Zikade, die Singzikaden *‚semi'* sind Insekten, die die meiste Zeit ihres Lebens als Larve in der Erde verbringen. Nach der Regenzeit krabbeln sie im Juni/Juli an die Oberfläche, schlüpfen und beginnen mit ihren Trommelorganen zu singen. Der schrille Klang tausender Zikaden kann sich wie Regen anhören.

To those asking

Ainu, indigenous people of northern Japan. Ainu means 'man' in Ainu language
Borrowed landscape, or '*shakkei*', describes how the surrounding scenery becomes part of a garden composition
Hot spring, '*onsen*', a place with hotels that have baths fed by natural hot springs.
Kamikaze, or **Shimp0 Tokkôtai** were suicide attacks by military aviators from the Empire of Japan against Allied naval vessels in the closing stages of the Pacific campaign of World War II.
Kimono, is a traditional Japanese kaftan style garment, which is held together by a wide belt (*'obi'*).
Nirvana flower, a lily variety blooming in September in Japan, and called ,'*higanbana*';in English 'flower from the other shore'. 'The other shore' is Nirvana, where worldly things are relinquished and replaced by enlightenment and non-material existence.
4'33'' (Four minutes, thirty-three seconds) is a piece of music of the avant-garde composer John Cage, in which not a single note is used.
Rice paper wall, movable room divider that features in the traditional architecture of Japan, used as external walls, doors or room dividers.
Plum blossoms, highly fragrant *'ume'*, the Japanese apricot or plum.
Sake, generally it refers to any kind of alcohol in Japan. Non-Japanese people tend to think of Japanese rice wine in first case.
Schönberg, Arnold (1874 – 1951) Jewish Austrian composer, emigrated to the United States, leader of the Second Viennese School and developer of the twelve-tone method of composition
Masaoka Shiki, (1867-1902) Japanese poet, writer, literary critic and essayist of the Meiji period, pioneer of modern haiku poetry, and one of the four great haiku masters, the others being Buson, Issa and Bashô
Shinkansen, is both the name of the stretch of Japanese high-speed railway and the name of the trains themselves
Sutra, literally 'thread' or 'chain', are the most elementary, mnemonic texts of Buddhism
Dry landscape garden, *'karesansui'*, is a special kind of Japanese garden, which consists only of gravel, stones and rocks. No plants are used except moss. Wavy patterns raked in gravel or sand surfaces indicate water.
Washi, handmade, translucent paper from Japan. It is made of bast fibers of low-growth woods (e.g. gampi and kozo).
Yamanote Line, ringroad line in Tôkyô and one of the most important and most frequented railway routes in the city.
Yosa Buson, (1716-1784) famous poet painter and one of the great haiku masters.
Yuzu, light yellow to orange, Japanese citrus fruit. It resembles the lemon but has a much more complex flavor.
Cicada, *'semi'* are insects that spend most of their lives as larvae in the soil. After the rainy season in June/July they crawl to the surface, hatch and begin to sing with their drum organs. The shrill sound of thousands of cicadas can sound like rain.

Dank
Acknowledgements

Gerda Förster für ihre anhaltende Unterstützung, Ermunterung und die wertvollen Rückmeldungen. Catherine Urquhart, die mit ihrem wundervollen poetischen Gespür geholfen hat, meine Übertragungen ins Englische zu schleifen. Gerd Börner, Ralf Bröcker und Dietmar Tauchner für ihre hilfreichen Hinweise. Dem Meguro International Haiku Circle, Tokyo, unter Leitung von Yasuomi Koganei, wo ich viele der hier gesammelten Haiku erstmals zu Gehör brachte.

Die Haiku (manchmal in einer etwas anderen Form) wurden in den folgenden Publikationen erstveröffentlicht: A Hundred Gourds, Asahi Haikuist Network, Chrysanthemum, Haiku Heute, Haiku-Jahrbuch 2013-2016, NHK Haiku Masters, Tageshaiku Blogspot, The Heron's Nest, The Mainichi Daily, Sommergras, WHA Haiga Contest.

The haiku (sometimes in a somewhat different form) were first published in the publications mentioned above.

My thanks to Gerda Förster for her continued support, encouragement and valuable feedback. Catherine Urquhart, who has helped to polish my English translations with her marvellous poetic sense. Gerd Börner, Ralf Bröcker and Dietmar Tauchner for their helpful tips. The Meguro International Haiku Circle, Tokyo, under the direction of Yasuomi Koganei, where many haiku in this collection were presented for the first time.

Simone K. Busch

1965 in Berlin geboren; lebt in der Nähe von Bonn
Industriekauffrau und Diplom Betriebswirtin
Referentin für Personal- und Organisationsentwicklung
Weiterbildung zur Poesiepädagogin und Leitung von Schreibgruppen
Schreibt seit 2008 Haiku und gestaltet Foto-Haiku, zahlreiche Veröffentlichungen

Die Haiku und Fotografien in dieser Sammlung entstanden während eines vierjährigen Aufenthalts in Japan, in der Zeit von 2012-2016. Das Originalhaiku steht jeweils oben, die anderssprachige Version darunter. Auf die wortwörtliche Übertragung wurde zugunsten der bestmöglichen poetischen Ausdruckskraft in der jeweiligen Sprache verzichtet.

Born in Berlin, 1965; living close to Bonn
Master of Business Administration, Human Resources Advisor
Teacher of creative writing, leader of creative writing groups
Writing haiku and creating photo-haiku since 2008, numerous publishings

All haiku and photos were written and taken during a four-year stay in Japan (2012-2016). The original version precedes the German/English translation.

Simone K. Busch, Rheinbach im Januar 2017
Weighing Words, http://simonekbusch.blogspot.de